Astronauts in SPACE

FIRST EDITION
Project Editor Louise Pritchard; **Art Editor** Jill Plank; **Senior Editor** Linda Esposito; **Senior Art Editor** Diane Thistlethwaite; **US Editor** Regina Kahney; **Pre-Production Producer** Nadine King; **Producer** Sara Hu; **Picture Researcher** Andrea Sadler; **Illustrator** Peter Dennis; **Space Consultant** Carole Stott; **Indexer** Lynn Bresler; **Reading Consultant** Linda Gambrell, PhD

THIS EDITION
Editorial Management by Oriel Square
Produced for DK by WonderLab Group LLC
Jennifer Emmett, Erica Green, Kate Hale, *Founders*

Editors Grace Hill Smith, Libby Romero, Maya Myers, Michaela Weglinski;
Photography Editors Kelley Miller, Annette Kiesow, Nicole di Mella; **Managing Editor** Rachel Houghton;
Designers Project Design Company; **Researcher** Michelle Harris; **Copy Editor** Lori Merritt;
Indexer Connie Binder; **Proofreader** Larry Shea; **Reading Specialist** Dr. Jennifer Albro;
Curriculum Specialist Elaine Larson

Published in the United States by DK Publishing
1745 Broadway, 20th Floor, New York, NY 10019

Copyright © 2023 Dorling Kindersley Limited
DK, a Division of Penguin Random House LLC
23 24 25 26 10 9 8 7 6 5 4 3 2 1
001-333915-Oct/2023

All rights reserved.
Without limiting the rights under the copyright reserved above, no part of this publication may be reproduced, stored in or introduced into a retrieval system, or transmitted, in any form, or by any means (electronic, mechanical, photocopying, recording, or otherwise), without the prior written permission of the copyright owner.
Published in Great Britain by Dorling Kindersley Limited

A catalog record for this book
is available from the Library of Congress.
HC ISBN: 978-0-7440-7229-7
PB ISBN: 978-0-7440-7230-3

DK books are available at special discounts when purchased in bulk for sales promotions, premiums, fundraising, or educational use. For details, contact: DK Publishing Special Markets,
1745 Broadway, 20th Floor, New York, NY 10019
SpecialSales@dk.com

Printed and bound in China

The publisher would like to thank the following for their kind permission to reproduce their images:
a=above; c=center; b=below; l=left; r=right; t=top; b/g=background

Dreamstime.com: Mopic 6-7t, Noipornpan 8-9, Konstantin Shaklein / 3dsculptor 13bl; **Getty Images:** AFP / Stringer 17cr; **NASA:** 3, James Blair 11cr, Carla Cioffi 4-5, Bill Ingalls 7br, 13br, 28-29, 29cr, JSC 1, 9tl, 15cr, 16-17b, 19, 20-21b, 23tl, 23cra, 24cr, Shane Kimbrough 22t, Marshall Space Flight Center 10-11b, MSFC 23br, Kim Shiflett 14-15, 25t, SpaceX 12t, Reto Stckli, based on data from NASA and NOAA 7cr; **Shutterstock.com:** Dima Zel 19tl

Cover images: *Front:* **Shutterstock.com:** lexaarts; *Back:* **Shutterstock.com:** Jemastock bl, olegtoka cla, Pavlo Plakhotia cra

All other images © Dorling Kindersley
For more information see: www.dkimages.com

For the curious
www.dk.com

Level 3

Astronauts in SPACE

Kate Hayden and Roxanne Troup

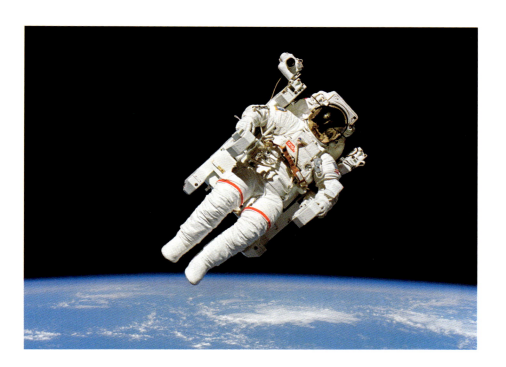

Contents

- **6**   Big, Blue Marble
- **8**   Becoming an Astronaut
- **12**   Blast Off!
- **16**   Living in Space

22 Working in Space
28 Returning to Earth
30 Glossary
31 Index
32 Quiz

Big, Blue Marble

From space, Earth looks like a giant, blue marble. White swirls of clouds float over huge oceans. Green and brown landforms dot the water. After sunset, city lights sparkle like diamonds. Astronauts on the International Space Station (ISS) see it all. They take pictures of Earth from their windows. Scientists will use the pictures to study everything from volcanoes to coral reefs.

The ISS is a science lab that orbits Earth. Russian and US space agencies began building it in 1998. Two years later, the space station welcomed its first crew. Since then, astronauts from all over the globe have lived onboard.

Christina Koch
Astronaut Christina Koch holds the record for the longest single spaceflight by a woman—328 days in space!

Becoming an Astronaut

Getting to the ISS isn't easy. Space agencies, like the National Aeronautics and Space Administration (NASA) in the United States, only choose a few people to train each year. These astronaut candidates have studied science, technology, engineering, and mathematics (STEM) for a long time. They have excellent critical thinking and problem-solving skills. These skills are necessary when you're far from home with limited supplies.

Space is hard on the human body. Before astronaut candidates are selected, they must pass several health tests. Doctors check their heart, lungs, eyes, and ears. People at NASA interview the final candidates. Then, they choose the men and women who will begin training.

The Right Fit

Astronauts must be between 62 and 75 inches (157–191 cm) tall. Otherwise, they won't fit in the space equipment!

Candidates spend up to two years training to become astronauts. They learn how to do things underwater, which feels a bit like being in space. They also train in simulators. A simulator is a program or machine that copies a real-life situation. It's a safe way to train someone to do the real thing.

Astronauts-in-training learn to do all the jobs they will need to do in space. They learn how to use equipment on the space station. They learn to repair telescopes. They even learn how to speak different languages so they can communicate with astronauts from other countries.

Practice Makes Perfect
Astronauts have to practice everything they will do in space—even eating and going to the bathroom.

Blast Off!

When it's time for a mission to begin, astronauts climb into the crew module and strap in. They wear special suits that protect their bodies from the dangers of spaceflight. They make final preparations and communicate with Launch Control as they wait for takeoff.

Going to Space
Astronauts have used a variety of spacecraft to travel to the ISS.

SPACE SHUTTLE
1981–2011

The clock begins to count down. "T minus 30 seconds" sounds over the radio. The countdown continues. Suddenly, a thundering ROAR shakes the launch pad. The rocket's engines ignite. Burning fuel bursts from under the rocket as hot air pushes against the ground.
The spacecraft lifts off.

SOYUZ SPACECRAFT
2000-Today

FALCON 9/DRAGON
2020-Today

Earth's gravity pulls down on the rocket as it climbs higher and higher into the sky. But the rocket's fuel is powerful. As it burns, it creates thrust. That force is greater than the pull of gravity. It pushes the rocket into orbit.

On Earth, Launch Control monitors takeoff. The spacecraft uses multistage rockets to launch into space. The rockets are stacked together. Each rocket contains an engine and fuel. As each stage of rocket runs out of fuel, it disconnects and drops into the ocean. The next stage takes over. Eventually, all that's left is the crew module. It carries the astronauts into space.

After separating, pieces of the SpaceX rocket return to Earth. They will be repaired and reused.

As the spacecraft nears the ISS, onboard sensors measure its distance, speed, and position. The spacecraft lines up for docking as it slowly approaches the space station. The two objects connect. The astronauts have arrived!

Flying to the Moon
A Saturn V rocket carried the spacecraft that took Apollo 11 astronauts Neil Armstrong, Edwin "Buzz" Aldrin, and Michael Collins to the Moon.

Living in Space

The ISS orbits around 250 miles (400 km) above Earth. It is about the size of an American football field. The space station has everything astronauts need to survive, but its main purpose is science. Everything astronauts learn onboard is used to help people on Earth or to make it possible for humans to live in space long-term.

Astronauts do many experiments in space. Their experiments get different results than they would on Earth. That's because there is less gravity in space. This condition of weak gravity is called microgravity. It causes astronauts—and everything else in space—to float!

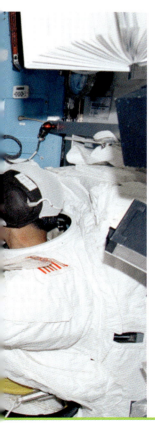

What's in a Name?
Astronauts are known by different names in different countries. In Russia, they are called cosmonauts. In China, they are called taikonauts or yuhangyuan.

An international crew of astronauts lives and works on the ISS year-round.

Floating in space might sound cool. But it does create challenges. How do you sleep when you can't stay on your bed? How do you eat when food floats off your plate? How do you wash your face when water floats in the air?

Before sending astronauts to space, NASA engineers had to solve these and many other problems. Their solutions worked. Astronauts have sleeping bags that attach to walls. They use Velcro to hold objects in place. Astronauts even have special food packages so they can eat and drink in space.

One thing that astronauts can't do on the ISS is take a bath. Liquids behave differently in space. On Earth, gravity makes water flow to the lowest point. But in space, water floats in bubble-like globs. Because of this, astronauts can't take baths or use showers or sinks. Instead, they use wet towels to wash.

Spotting the ISS
Sometimes, you can see the ISS as it circles Earth. It looks like a moving star.

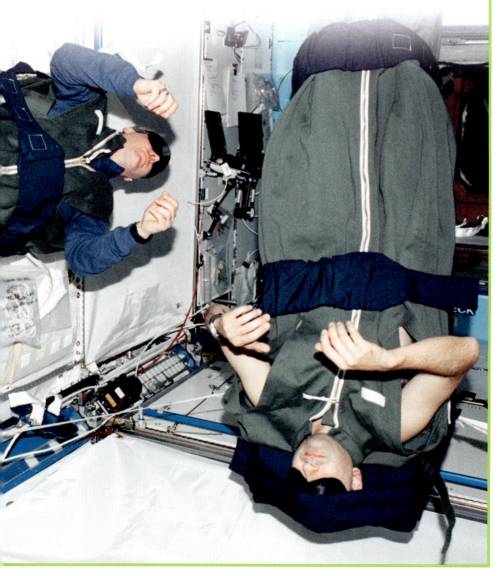

Like Earth, space is a dusty place. Dust can damage important machines onboard the ISS. Astronauts tackle that problem the same way we do on Earth—by doing chores.

The ISS has air filters that catch tiny dust particles, but astronauts still have to vacuum. They also have to wipe down surfaces to get rid of bacteria. A clean home keeps astronauts healthy and the ISS functioning well.

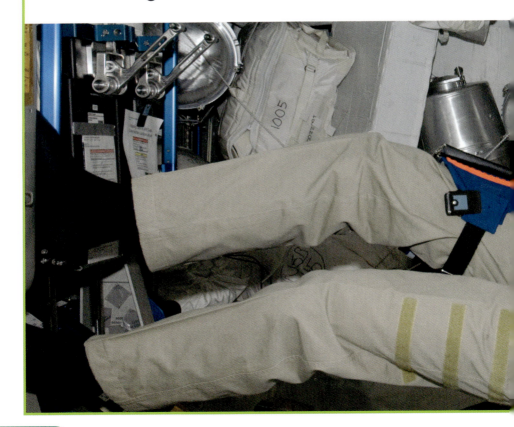

At the end of the day, astronauts take time to relax. They watch movies, play games, and even call home. Some astronauts use amateur, or ham, radio to talk with people on Earth. Amateur Radio on the International Space Station (ARISS) is a fun way to learn from on-the-job astronauts.

21

Working in Space

Astronauts follow a strict schedule. Everything they do in space—eating, working, taking breaks, and sleeping—is on the schedule. To keep things rolling, Mission Control lets astronauts know when it's time to wake up. Music and "good morning" messages play throughout the space station.

After the astronauts have cleaned up and eaten their breakfast, it's time to go to work. They spend most of their day working on experiments. Some experiments test new technologies, like the Astrobee.

Astrobees help astronauts do their jobs on the ISS.

Robots in Space
NASA tests robots on the ISS to learn how to make smarter robots. Eventually, these robots could help people explore other planets.

Astrobees are cube-shaped robots that fly around the ISS. Each one is about the size of a toaster. These little robots were designed to do things like track inventory or film astronauts as they do experiments. They can even find lost pieces of equipment. Astrobees can fly on their own or be controlled with a remote.

Astronauts do lots of experiments. Some experiments are designed to improve life for people living on Earth. For example, astronauts test medicines and investigate how concrete hardens in space. Astronauts also monitor glaciers, coral reefs, and other landforms to help researchers on Earth understand how the planet is changing.

Safety First!
Sometimes, astronauts experiment with dangerous materials. To keep everyone safe, the ISS has two special labs called gloveboxes that are sealed tight so nothing escapes.

To help people learn how to live in space, astronauts research new ways to grow food on the ISS. They test different kinds of seeds, and they try to find new ways to grow vegetables without soil. The best part comes when the experiment is over. They get to eat what they grow!

Part of an astronaut's job is to repair things on the ISS when they break. Fixing equipment inside the space station is one thing. But what happens when something breaks down outside?

Sometimes, astronauts use a giant, remote-controlled robotic arm called Canadarm2. This robotic technician has "hands" that can grab and move things. It can even catch unpiloted cargo ships coming in for a landing. The "hands" can also attach to special fixtures on the outside of the ISS. Canadarm2 walks end over end, reattaching itself with each step.

To complete some repairs, astronauts must go outside the space station. They wear special suits called extravehicular mobility units, or EMUs. EMUs protect astronauts' bodies from the extreme hot and cold of space. The suits carry oxygen. Their helmets have headphones and a microphone so crew members can communicate.

Returning to Earth

Most astronauts stay onboard the ISS for six months. After a mission is complete, returning home is both exciting and dangerous. Earth is surrounded by a blanket of gas called atmosphere. Spacecraft must reenter Earth's atmosphere at the right angle and speed. Objects will burn up if they enter Earth's atmosphere at an angle that is too steep. If the angle is too shallow, they will skip off the atmosphere and stay in space.

Rescue boats wait for returning astronauts near the splash zone.

As a spacecraft approaches Earth, a computer program slows it down and guides it home. Once it is through Earth's atmosphere, giant parachutes open. They make it go even slower. Soon, the spacecraft splashes into the ocean. The astronauts are home!

Beat the Heat
Friction causes objects to burn as they go through Earth's atmosphere. A heat shield protects returning spacecraft and the people inside.

Glossary

Astronaut
A person trained to travel in a spacecraft

Atmosphere
A blanket of gases that surrounds Earth

Docking
Connecting with another spacecraft while in space

Friction
A force that slows or stops movement between two objects when they rub against each other

Gravity
An invisible force of attraction that pulls objects toward the center of Earth

International Space Station (ISS)
An international science lab in space

Launch Control
The group of people on the ground that monitors the takeoff of a spacecraft

Mission
A journey into space to gather scientific information

Mission Control
The group of people on the ground that monitors a spaceflight from launch to the final landing

Microgravity
The condition where very weak gravity causes people or objects to appear to be weightless

Orbit
To move around something

Simulator
A program or machine that stands in for a real-life situation during training

STEM
An abbreviation for science, technology, engineering, and mathematics; often used in education

Thrust
A force that pushes things forward or upward

Index

Aldrin, Edwin "Buzz" 15

Apollo 11 15

Armstrong, Neil 15

Astrobees 22–23

atmosphere 28–29

becoming an astronaut 8–11

blast off 12–15

Canadarm2 27

chores 20

Collins, Michael 15

crew module 12, 14

docking 15

dust 20

Earth, from space 6

eating and drinking 18

experiments 17, 22–24

extravehicular mobility units (EMUs) 27

food 18, 25

friction 29

gravity 14, 17, 18

growing food 25

human body 8

Koch, Christina 7

Launch Control 12, 14

living in space 16–21

microgravity 17

Mission Control 22

Moon 15

orbit 7, 14, 16

returning to Earth 28–29

robotic arm 27

robots 23

rockets 13, 14, 15

Saturn V rocket 15

simulators 10

spacesuits 12, 27

SpaceX rocket 14

thrust 14

training 10–11

working in space 22–27

31

Quiz

Answer the questions to see what you have learned. Check your answers in the key below.

1. Why do astronauts go to the International Space Station?
2. What do many people study before becoming astronauts?
3. How long does astronaut training last?
4. What causes astronauts and everything else to float in space?
5. What do astronauts use to hold objects in place when they are in space?
6. Why can't astronauts use showers and sinks in space?
7. What kind of suit does an astronaut wear to go outside a spacecraft?
8. What causes objects to burn as they go through Earth's atmosphere?

1. To learn how people can live and work in space 2. Science, technology, engineering, and mathematics (STEM) 3. Up to two years 4. Microgravity 5. Velcro 6. Water floats in bubble-like globs in space 7. Extravehicular mobility unit (EMU) 8. Friction